Autumn
Daily
Devotional
for Women

Esther Ellison

to

....

From

....

Note & Date

....

....

Table of Contents

Table of Contents

Disclaimer and Legal Notice

Introduction: Autumn Reset, Everyday Joy

As the leaves turn and the air sharpens, this season invites us to pause, reset, and rediscover joy in the everyday. These devotions are written to meet you right where you are: in busy schedules, anxious nights, or distracted moments. They are here to guide you toward gratitude, rest, and sturdy hope.

How to use this book: Read one entry per day, five days per week. Keep it simple with short readings, short prayers, and short reflections. What matters most is showing up with consistency, not perfection. If you miss a day, simply begin again. There is no pressure here.

If this book was given to you as a gift, remember what a beautiful thing it is that someone cared enough to find this for you. They wanted you to be encouraged and strengthened in your walk with God. If you chose it for yourself, that speaks to the value you place on your spiritual growth and on caring for your own heart.

And here's something fun. Throughout the book you will find 4 easter eggs that are on one page each. Let's see if you can find them all. If you do, you can email us the names of the items at contact.greenhopex@gmail.com

 and we will send you our next book for free before release.

This devotional is just one part of our journey together. We have created other meaningful and beautiful devotionals that will inspire and uplift you. Be sure to visit our author page to discover more.

Day 1: First Light in a Crisp Morning

"This is the day the Lord has made; let us rejoice and be glad in it." (Psalm 118:24)

The alarm went off while the sky was still blue-gray. My hand reached for my phone before my feet reached the floor. One swipe turned into three, then five, and suddenly I was reading about storms in cities far from mine, a celebrity breakup, and a sale I did not need. My stomach tightened. The sun slipped through the blinds, but my heart already felt behind.

I shuffled to the kitchen, set the kettle on, and noticed my thumb hovering, ready to open another app. I caught myself and stepped to the back door. The air was crisp and clean, like the world had been washed overnight. A neighbor's maple tree looked like glowing embers. My breath puffed in little clouds. In that quiet, a sentence rose up in me, gentle and steady. This is the day the Lord has made.

Not tomorrow with its lists. Not yesterday with its mistakes. This one.

I whispered it out loud, then added, "I will rejoice and be glad." It felt small, but it was a choice. The kettle hummed. I wrapped both hands around my mug and named three gifts before I touched my phone. Warm ceramic. The faint scent of cinnamon from yesterday's toast. The sound of a mourning dove. My shoulders dropped. The news still existed, but it did not get the first word.

Doomscrolling had trained my heart to expect trouble before breakfast. No wonder mornings felt frantic and thin. I decided to change the script with one simple tweak. I plugged my phone in the hallway and set an old alarm clock on my nightstand. I put a sticky note on the kettle that said, "Start with God." I laid my Bible and a pen on the table, open to a page with room to write three lines.

The next morning, the habit tried to pull me back. My hand still twitched, but the note on the kettle met me like a friend. I stood at the door again, breathing in the cool, naming what I could see, touch, and hear. Before long, my mind felt less cluttered. The day felt like a gift I was unwrapping, not a flood I was resisting.

Begin with the gift of today before your feed defines it. The feed can come later. First, let the Maker set the tone.

Prayer

"Lord, this day is Yours. Train my eyes to notice Your gifts." Teach me to start with Your voice and Your kindness. Guard my mind from noise, and help me choose simple habits that make room for joy. Let gratitude be my first word, not worry. Amen.

A Moment with God

What three good things already present this morning will I name before breakfast?

Day 2: Be Still as Leaves Settle

"Be still, and know that I am God." (Psalm 46:10)

By 9 a.m., I had already lost count of the tabs open in my head. Reply to that email. Sign the permission slip. Check the calendar. Add milk to the list. The thoughts zigzagged like leaves in a gust, never landing. My shoulders felt tight and my jaw ached from clenching. I told myself to push through, to be productive, but the more I pushed, the foggier my brain became.

On my way to make coffee, I stopped at the window. A single golden leaf loosened and floated down. It twirled, paused, sank, then settled to the ground. I felt God's nudge. Be still, just for a moment.

I set a timer for thirty seconds. That was all. I closed my eyes, relaxed my hands, and breathed in slowly. In. Out. I imagined the leaf sinking. My thoughts kept trying to sprint. I did not fight them. I let them drift by like cars on a road, and I returned my attention to God with one simple sentence. You are here.

The timer chimed. I was surprised by the difference. My pulse had slowed. The things I needed to do were still there, but they no longer shouted. I could choose the next right thing with a clearer mind.

Thirty seconds felt almost silly, yet it was enough to turn my heart from scattered to steady. I decided to anchor this pause to places I could not miss. Kettle on, pause. Car in park, pause. Before I open my laptop, pause. I even put a tiny leaf sticker on the corner of my screen to remind me. Be still as the leaves settle, then act.

Over the week, those little pauses stitched peace into busy places. When a text pinged during dinner, I breathed and remembered who was at my table. When the to-do list felt like a wave, I let my soul sit with God for one minute and remembered He is God, not me. My plans do not hold the world together. He does.

Thirty seconds of stillness slows your nervous system and recenters your plans on God's presence. It is small, but it is holy.

Prayer

"God, still my racing thoughts and anchor me in You." Teach me to pause before I perform, to breathe before I react. In the quiet, remind me that You are God and I am held. Make stillness my doorway to wisdom today. Amen.

A Moment with God

Where will I place a daily 60-second stillness stop so it actually happens?

Day 3: Shoofly Pie and Truth

"Whatever is true, whatever is noble, whatever is right, whatever is pure, whatever is lovely... think about such things." (Philippians 4:8)

The morning sunlight spilled across my kitchen table, catching the steam rising from a mug of coffee. For a moment I felt steady and grateful, reminded that beauty often lives in the simplest places. Life is full of good gifts if only I pause to notice them: the laughter of my children, the hum of a quiet house, the promise of another new day.

But that steady feeling can vanish quickly. One quick scroll on my phone and I find myself lost in a maze. Perfect pumpkin patch photos. A stranger's remodel. Hot takes about topics I barely understand. Each image pulls me toward envy or irritation, convincing me that my own life is smaller, duller, or somehow less. By the time I set my phone down, my soup has nearly boiled over and my mood has already sunk.

It was then I remembered gardens. In fall, you prune on purpose. You cut back what is overgrown so the plant can stay healthy. My mind needed the same kind of pruning. If I kept feeding on endless comparison, my spirit would wither. Philippians 4:8 came to life for me: fix your thoughts on what is true, noble, right, pure, and lovely. I needed to filter my inputs so my soul could feast on what nourished, not what drained.

This realization made me think of my granny's shoofly pie. At first glance it seemed plain compared to frosted cakes or glossy tarts, but one bite told a deeper story. Rich molasses, crumbly topping, and honest sweetness filled you more than you expected. It was not flashy, but it was good. Just like that pie, God's truth often comes quiet and steady, enough to satisfy if I choose it.

Now I am learning to prune the noise and feed on what lasts. A muted account here, a verse taped to the fridge there, and slowly my days taste different. When I open my Bible before I open my apps, I find that my soul settles. God's feast is never junk food. Like Granny's shoofly pie, it may look simple, but it is rich with the kind of sweetness that endures. Here is our recipe below. May our tradition enrich your family too.

Prayer

"Spirit, turn my attention toward what is true and good." Guard my eyes from envy and my mind from cynicism. Help me prune with wisdom, and fill what I remove with Your words and beauty. Shape my feed and my heart to love what You love. Amen.

A Moment with God

What is one life-giving voice I can add to my daily feed? And one to mute?

My Grannys Shoofly Pie

Servings	Prep Time	Cook time
8	15'	45'

Nutritional Info (per serving)
Calories: 455 kcal | Protein: 4 g|
Sodium: 249 mg | Fat: 14 g | Carbs: 85 g
| Cholesterol: 23mg

INGREDIENTS
- 1 cup molasses
- 3/4 cup hot water
- 3/4 TSP baking soda
- 1 egg, beaten
- 1 (9-inch) deep dish pie crust
- 1 ½ cups flour (all-purpose)
- 1 cup packed brown sugar
- 1/4 cup shortening

DIRECTIONS
1. Preheat. Preheat the oven to 400°F (200°C) and place a rack in the center.
2. In a medium bowl, whisk together the molasses, hot water, and baking soda. Add the beaten egg and whisk until smooth. Pour into the unbaked deep-dish pie shell
3. Crumb Topping. In another bowl, mix the flour and brown sugar. Cut in the shortening (or butter) with a fork until the mixture looks like coarse crumbs
4. Assemble. Sprinkle the crumb mixture evenly over the molasses filling
5. Bake. Place the pie on a baking sheet and bake for 15 minutes. Without removing, reduce the oven temperature to 350°F (175°C) and continue baking until the filling is set, about 30 minutes more.
6. Cool. Let the pie cool completely before slicing. Serve plain or with whipped cream.

Day 4: Harvest Eyes

"You crown the year with Your bounty; Your paths overflow with abundance." (Psalm 65:11-13)

All week I had felt behind. Behind on emails, behind on laundry, behind on the goals I wrote last January. The trees outside shouted harvest, yet my heart kept whispering not enough. On Thursday, I stumbled over this verse. You crown the year with Your bounty. I paused. Maybe the problem was not a lack of fruit. Maybe I needed harvest eyes.

I opened a small notebook and wrote "Evidence List" at the top. Not big miracles, just small answers. I asked, "What has God already done?" The first lines came slow. Then they came easier. A friend texted at the exact moment I felt lonely. The car started even though the battery had been weak. My child's fever broke overnight. A bill was lower than expected. A neighbor brought over apple muffins just because she baked too many.

Each line was a seed of joy. My circumstances did not change, yet my posture did. I started noticing how God's paths overflow in quiet ways. The problem solved before I saw it. The right person in the right place. The sunset that painted the whole street gold.

I kept the notebook on the counter and added to it while the pasta boiled or the coffee dripped. By the weekend, the page was full. The list did not erase the hard parts, but it reminded me I was not walking alone or empty. God was not stingy. He was steady and generous, even in small things.

Gratitude moved from theory to sight. When cynicism tried to creep in, I read the lines out loud. You crowned this week with bits of bounty. I will not miss the harvest because I was staring at the weeds.

God crowns the year with bounty. Keep an evidence list of small answers. The more you record, the more you will recognize.

Prayer

"Thank You for what You have already done. Make me watchful." Open my eyes to Your faithful fingerprints in ordinary hours. Help me receive small gifts as real grace. Turn my heart from scarcity to trust, from grumbling to wonder. Teach me to count what counts. Amen.

A Moment with God

What three recent "small answers" deserve a line in my evidence list?

Day 5: Set the Sabbath Table

"Remember the Sabbath day, to keep it holy." (Exodus 20:8)

*E*very Sunday I said I wanted rest, yet I carried a knot of guilt. Church was good, but the hours after felt like catch-up. Laundry piles, grocery runs, stray emails. I called it Sabbath, but it felt like a messy hallway between busy weeks.

One Saturday afternoon, I remembered my grandmother's table. Nothing fancy. A simple soup simmered, a clean corner, a candle waiting. She did a little work beforehand so Sunday could breathe. Rest is prepared. That line landed in me like a key.

I chose one pot of soup for Saturdays. Carrots, onions, broth, and herbs. I cleared a small corner of the living room, stacked the unread mail elsewhere, put a soft blanket on the chair, and set a candle on the table with a match beside it. I silenced notifications on my phone and slid it into a drawer. Two ten-minute tasks made the space ready. Sweep the floor. Load the dishwasher.

The next day, Sabbath felt different. We came home, lit the candle, and warmed the soup. The house was not perfect, but the corner was peaceful and ready. We read, we napped, we took a slow walk under rustling trees. The guilt untied itself because I was not performing. I was receiving.

By evening, I felt fuller than I had in weeks. Not because I did nothing, but because I made room to delight. Rest stopped being a vague idea and became a table set for God and my soul.

Rest is prepared. A simple Saturday soup and a tidy corner turn Sabbath from idea into reality. Make the preparation light, then enter the gift.

Prayer

"Lord of rest, help me prepare to delight, not perform." Show me simple steps that make space for joy. Protect my Sabbath from hurry and from guilt. Let my home hold peace, and let my heart learn to receive it with gratitude. Amen.

A Moment with God

What two ten-minute tasks tonight will set a restful Sabbath table tomorrow?

Day 6: Stay Inside Today

"Therefore do not worry about tomorrow, for tomorrow will worry about itself. Each day has enough trouble of its own." (Matthew 6:34)

The first cold snap of fall arrived, and so did my racing thoughts. I stood at the kitchen sink, watching yellow leaves skate across the driveway, and my brain sprinted three days ahead. What about that meeting? What if the bill is higher than we planned? Should I change my doctor appointment? I could feel my chest tighten, like someone cinched a belt around my ribs. I kept stacking tomorrow on top of today until the pile swayed.

I grabbed my planner to feel in control, but the pages turned into a flood. The list looked like a maze. My joy felt far away, like a porch light in fog. I remembered Jesus' words. He did not say I had to fix next week. He said today has enough. Joy lives in 24-hour containers. It is like God hands me a small basket every morning. It holds enough grace for this sunrise to bedtime, not for next Thursday.

So I shrank my world to the size of a day. I wrote on a sticky note: Just today. Under it, I listed one next single step. Not the whole project, just the next tiny move. Send the email, not plan the whole event. Put chicken in the sink to thaw, not solve dinner for the month. Set a timer for ten minutes to start the laundry, not conquer Mount Clothes.

I put my phone in a drawer and took three slow breaths by the window. The oak tree swayed. My shoulders dropped. I whispered, God, keep me inside today. The knot in my stomach loosened. The problems did not vanish, but their edges softened. I could hear the kettle click off and the clock tick. I could actually taste my tea.

By noon, I had taken three next steps. Nothing flashy. No perfect plan. Just faithfulness inside today's fence. The surprise was how light it felt. Not easy, but lighter. I realized I had been dragging tomorrow into today. No wonder I was exhausted. Jesus was not asking me to carry two days at once. He was inviting me to receive the grace sized for this one. Shrinking today did not shrink my life. It made space for joy to breathe.

Prayer

Father, keep me inside today's boundaries. Train my heart to release tomorrow into Your hands and receive the grace You have portioned for this sunrise to tonight. Give me clarity for the next single step, courage to take it, and peace to stop when today is full. Amen.

A Moment with God

What problem am I dragging from tomorrow into today, and what is the next single step only?

Day 7: Candle and Quiet

"He makes me lie down in green pastures. He leads me beside still waters. He restores my soul." (Psalm 23:2–3)

By October, my brain starts buzzing like a hive. Lists on the fridge, carpool times, a calendar full of boxes. One afternoon the sky turned soft gray, and the house felt loud even when it was quiet. I lit a small cinnamon candle and sat in the old chair by the window. Ten minutes, I told myself. No phone. Just breathe and let my eyes rest on the maple tree out front.

At first, my thoughts fidgeted. Did I reply to that text? What about dinner? The candle's tiny flame flickered. The maple leaves dangled like little hands waving. My heart slowed. I could hear the distant hum of traffic and the steady rhythm of my own breath. It felt like stepping off a rushing treadmill and standing on grass.

I used to think restoration required a retreat or a perfect morning routine. Today, the Shepherd reminded me He restores in small, local places. A slow fall walk. A chair by a window. The hush of a library aisle. The warm porch steps in late sun. These are pastures for modern hearts. Ten minutes can feel like a lot when your mind is frayed, yet it is enough for God to lay you down inside His care.

So I made a plan as simple as soup. Pick a daily pasture. Name it. Schedule it like a meeting with the One who knows my soul. My pasture would be the chair with the candle at 3:30, after school drop-off, before dinner duties start. I set a small timer and left my phone in the kitchen. On days when rain kept me inside, the window became my still waters. On better days, I walked the neighborhood loop, crunching leaves and listening for birds.

Here is what surprised me. After ten quiet minutes, I did not feel lazy. I felt clear. My thoughts unknotted. Decisions that felt tangled in the morning loosened. I could smile at the noise again. God was not asking me to power through the valley. He was inviting me to lie down on purpose, to let Him put restoration back in my bones.

Prayer

Shepherd, lead me beside still waters. Teach me to pause before I snap, to sit before I spiral. Meet me in small, simple places and restore my soul. Mark my day with Your quiet so I can carry Your peace back into the noise. Amen.

A Moment with God

Which 10-minute "pasture" will I visit daily this week and when?

Your feedback is a true blessing!

If this book has encouraged you or helped you feel less alone, would you leave a quick review?

Even one sentence makes a huge difference and takes just a minute. As a small author, your feedback not only lifts my heart... it also helps other women of faith with find the support and hope they need.

Thank you for being part of this journey!

Scan this QR code with your phone to go to the review page

Or

Go to your orders, find the book and click

"Write a product review"

Thank you <3

Day 8: Trust Over Tangles

"Trust in the Lord with all your heart, and do not lean on your own understanding. In all your ways acknowledge Him, and He will make straight your paths." (Proverbs 3:5–6)

The email sat in my inbox like a knot. A new opportunity sounded good on paper, but it tangled everything else. What if I say yes and regret it? What if I say no and miss God's best? I opened a spreadsheet to weigh pros and cons. My head hurt. My heart felt even worse. Decision fatigue is not just tired thinking. It is soul weariness from trying to control outcomes I cannot see.

While washing dishes, I remembered the promise. God makes paths straight. He did not promise perfect outcomes or zero bumps. He promised direction. Straight does not mean smooth. It means aligned with Him. I dried my hands and prayed aloud, simple words in a small kitchen. Jesus, I trust You with what I cannot untie. Show me the next right step.

I decided to shift my goal. Not certainty, but clarity for today. I wrote one question in my journal: What would faith do right now? Then I listed two people known for wisdom and calm. Not friends who echo my fears, but voices who love Scripture and tell the truth. I sent a message asking for input within 48 hours. I set a deadline so I could stop spinning. I asked God for one confirming sign of peace, not a lightning bolt, just a steady sense that matches His Word and wise counsel.

By evening, I felt lighter. The situation had not changed, but my posture had. I was not yanking at the knot. I was handing Him the rope. The next day, both advisors pointed to the same step. It was not flashy. It was faithful. I took it. The path did not jump to the finish line, but it did feel straight enough for my feet.

That is the secret I keep relearning. Ask for straight paths, not perfect outcomes. Ask for a lamp for your feet, not a floodlight for the whole highway. God loves guiding hearts that surrender. He meets you where you stand, clears the next few feet, and walks it with you.

Prayer

Jesus, I trust You with what I cannot untie. Quiet my urge to control and teach me to obey the light I have. Align my steps with Your wisdom. Bring the right counsel at the right time and give me courage to move when You make the path straight. Amen.

A Moment with God

What decision needs surrender, and whose wise input will I seek within 48 hours?

Day 9: He Gives Sleep

"It is in vain that you rise up early and go late to rest, eating the bread of anxious toil, for He gives to His beloved sleep." (Psalm 127:2)

I used to treat sleep like a reward I had to earn. One more email. One more sink to scrub. One more scroll to numb my mind. Then midnight would stare back, and my body felt wired, not tired. The next day my patience was thin and my faith felt flimsy. Anxiety grew in the cracks.

One evening I decided to try a gentler way. If God gives sleep, maybe I could practice receiving it. I set a small alarm for thirty minutes before my target bedtime. When it chimed, I told myself, Work is closed. I dimmed the lamps to signal evening to my brain. I brewed chamomile and took a warm shower. I stretched my shoulders and neck. I wrote down three lingering worries in a notebook and prayed them into His hands. I left the notebook outside the bedroom as a sign that I did not have to sleep with my problems.

I made the room cool and dark. I put my phone in the kitchen to charge. I told the to-do list, You can wait for tomorrow's grace. Then I read one Psalm slowly, like a lullaby for a tired heart. My breath deepened. Sleep came like a tide.

The world did not end because I stopped. In fact, I woke up clearer. It struck me that sleep is trust in a practical form. I am not the keeper of the universe. I do not have to hold every spinning plate. God stays awake, so I do not have to. A gentle wind-down beats one more task, because it opens my hands to receive what He loves to give.

This is not about perfection. Some nights still feel squirrelly. On those nights, I repeat a breath prayer. Inhale, Beloved Giver. Exhale, I rest in You. Two simple cues anchor me: dim lights, warm shower. Tiny signals that say to my body, You are safe. You can stop now. Peace grows in that quiet place, and joy follows close behind.

Prayer

Beloved Giver, teach me to stop in peace. Help me honor my limits, close the day with trust, and receive the gift of sleep without guilt. Set a gentle rhythm in my evenings so my body and mind remember that You are God and I am held. Amen.

A Moment with God

Which two cues will form my 20-minute wind-down tonight?

Day 10: Cast, Do Not Clutch

"Cast all your anxiety on Him because He cares for you." (1 Peter 5:7)

I did not notice how tight my hands were until my daughter asked, Why do your knuckles look white? I laughed, then realized I had been gripping my worries like a rope that burns. Money questions. A friend's silence. A test result not here yet. I prayed about them, but I also kept snatching them back, like a boomerang of fear.

One Saturday we walked by the river. The trees wore gold, and the water moved with quiet strength. I picked up a smooth stone and felt God nudge my heart. Cast, do not clutch. I wrote a single worry on the rock with a chalk marker. Then I prayed aloud, simple and honest. I cast this care on You: the medical result. I threw the stone. It splashed and vanished. The problem did not end, but the grip in my chest loosened.

Since then I have practiced a physical transfer. Sometimes I write worries on scrap paper, pray them out loud, and toss them in the trash. Sometimes I drop a pebble in a jar on my desk. Sometimes I open my palms and breathe slowly, picturing my care moving into God's strong hands. It feels childlike, and it helps. My body learns what my heart believes. He cares for me. He carries what I cannot.

Casting is not passivity. After I release, I do the next faithful action. Make the call. Send the apology. Step into the small obedience in front of me. But I refuse to clutch the rest. I let God be God while I be loved. That shift brings real relief, the kind that lets joy return to the room.

Today, try it. Name one care out loud. Place it into His hands with a simple, physical act. Feel the difference between tight fists and open palms. You are not built to be a vault for fear. You are invited to be a child who trusts.

Prayer

I cast this care on You: _____. Father, I release what I cannot control and receive Your steady love. Teach my body and mind to unclench, to let You carry what weighs me down, and to do the next faithful step with a quiet heart. Amen.

A Moment with God

What worry will I write, pray aloud, and discard today?

Day 11: Spouse as Gift

"Nevertheless let every one of you in particular so love his wife even as himself, and the wife see that she reverence her husband." (Ephesians 5:33)

I woke up already annoyed. The sink held two cereal bowls, a wet towel hugged the bathroom floor, and his gym bag sat like a lazy dog by the doorway. My thoughts lined up like a row of pointing fingers. Why does he never put things away? Why am I always the one seeing the mess? I sighed loud enough for him to hear.

"Morning," he said, handing me coffee.

"Morning," I answered, clipped and cool. He went quiet. I felt that familiar slide into the criticism cycle. I point out a flaw, he withdraws, I feel alone, so I point again. By lunch we are roommates sharing Wi-Fi, not hearts.

That afternoon, while switching a load of laundry, I found a wrinkled receipt tucked in his pocket. It was for my favorite candles and a note scribbled on the back: "For tonight. Porch time." He had planned something kind. My eyes stung. I had been so busy counting his misses that I missed his love.

That verse from Ephesians nudged me. Love and respect are not payment for perfection. They are choices that create closeness. Appreciation interrupts fault-finding. I whispered a simple goal. Today, I will thank him for three concrete things, out loud.

First, while he fixed the wobbly chair I said, "Thank you for keeping our home working." His face softened. Later, when he made eggs for the kids, I added, "I see how you care for them." After dinner on the porch, I touched his arm. "Thank you for planning this. You know me."

The air between us warmed. We did not solve every habit or mess, but the tone changed. Respect made space for love to breathe. The next morning I stuck a tiny note on the coffee maker: "Interrupt the critic." It became my rule. When I feel the urge to point out a flaw, I pause and name a gift. Not fake flattery. Real, specific thanks. It is amazing how often I can find one when I look.

Seeing your spouse as a gift does not erase problems. It resets the atmosphere so problems can be handled with kindness instead of contempt. I still ask for what I need. I still say, "Please hang the towel." But now the first word I reach for is gratitude. And gratitude invites him closer.

Prayer

Lord, soften my tone and sharpen my gratitude. Teach me to see my spouse as your good gift, not a project to fix. Guard my mouth from fault-finding, and fill my heart with specific thanks that build trust, joy, and warmth in our home. Help us choose closeness, again and again. Amen.

A Moment with God

Which three qualities will I thank my spouse for this week, and how?

Day 12: Olive Shoots Table

"Thy wife shall be as a fruitful vine by the sides of thine house: thy children like olive plants round about thy table." (Psalm 128:3)

I wanted a picture-perfect dinner. The kind with cloth napkins, roasted chicken, and candles that make everything feel special. Instead the baby was fussy, the middle one spilled sauce across the table like a red river, and the oldest was hunting for a missing math worksheet. My jaw tightened. The little voice in my head started its lecture. You should do better. Other moms manage this.

Then I heard it. A small laugh. The fussy baby calmed when his big sister put a carrot stick behind her ear and crossed her eyes. The oldest handed the middle one a paper towel like a superhero cape. They were messy and loud, but they were alive. Olive shoots. Growing, not perfect.

That verse painted a deeper picture than the one on my phone screen. The blessing is not a flawless table. The blessing is life around it. Growth is slow. Olive trees do not rush. They stretch ring by ring, watered by daily faithfulness.

So we tried something new. Ten minutes. That was our goal. No gourmet meal required. We set a timer, lit one candle even if pizza was in a box, and played a simple round of "rose, thorn, bud." Rose is the best part of your day, thorn is the hard part, bud is what you are looking forward to tomorrow. The baby babbled his own version. The middle one said her rose was the dog licking her sock. The oldest said his thorn was the lost worksheet, then smiled when I said we would find it together after we ate.

Those ten minutes felt like an anchor. I stopped chasing perfect and started noticing life. I saw how my husband's tired eyes brightened when someone thanked him for picking up milk. I noticed the tiny jokes that only our family understands. The candle glow looked almost like a blessing sitting right there in the middle of spilled sauce and paper plates.

Mom guilt loosened its grip. The goal was not a magazine spread. The goal was warmth. The fruit of a family grows in small, steady rituals. Ten minutes can hold a lot of love.

Prayer

Father, help me treasure the life in my home. Open my eyes to the small smiles, the silly jokes, the little wins that prove growth is happening. Teach me to protect simple rhythms that nourish our hearts, even on messy days. Thank you for the gift of our table. Amen.

A Moment with God

What 10-minute family ritual will I protect this week?

Day 13: Russian Tea and Honest Friends

"Iron sharpeneth iron; so a man sharpeneth the countenance of his friend."
(Proverbs 27:17)

Fall has a way of stirring hope. The air cools, leaves scatter under our feet, and the colors remind us that change can be beautiful. In the same way, God weaves beauty into our friendships. A word spoken at the right time, or the presence of someone who cares, can lift our spirits and remind us that we are not walking alone. Friendship, when rooted in His Word, becomes a gift that steadies our hearts.

Still, silence often slips in. A misunderstanding, a forgotten call, or careless words can create distance. We tell ourselves it is easier to pull away, but deep down, we long for connection. God never intended us to walk in isolation. He designed friendship to be the place where honesty and grace meet, where love is courageous enough to speak and humble enough to listen.

Iron sharpens iron. The process may create sparks, but it is not meant to harm. It is meant to refine. When a friend speaks truth in love, it may feel uncomfortable in the moment, but it draws us closer to God and closer to one another. Honest love deepens peace more than silence ever could. True friendship holds up a mirror, not to condemn us, but to help us shine.

In our home, fall also means Russian Tea. The spiced aroma rises in the steam, filling the kitchen and drawing family together. Around that table, laughter is shared, stories are told, and space is made for even the harder words. The warmth of that cup is an invitation, reminding us that friendships grow when we gather, listen, and speak with love. Just as the tea welcomes us in, may our lives become an open invitation to others, offering a place where kindness and truth are served freely.

Prayer

God, make me a friend who sharpens with kindness and listens with humility. Keep me from building quiet walls. Instead, let my words carry warmth, like a shared cup of tea, drawing others closer to You and to one another. Amen.

A Moment with God

Who can I invite into friendship this week with both encouragement and truth spoken in love?

Sweet Russian Tea

Servings	Prep Time	Cook time
16	15'	25'
1 Gallon		

Nutritional Info (per serving)
Calories: 129 kcal | Protein: 0 g|
Sodium: 8 mg | Fat: 0 g | Carbs: 30 g |
Cholesterol: 0mg

INGREDIENTS
- 1 gallon water, divided
- 4 family-size black tea bags
- 1 ½ to 2 cups honey, adjusted to taste
- 1 cinnamon stick
- 1 teaspoon whole cloves
- 2 cups pineapple juice
- 2 cups orange juice
- ¼ cup lemon juice

DIRECTIONS
1. Boil two quarts of water, remove from heat, and steep the tea bags for twenty minutes. Discard the bags.
2. In another pot, heat the remaining two quarts of water with honey, cinnamon, and cloves until the honey dissolves and the spices are fragrant.
3. Stir in the brewed tea, pineapple juice, orange juice, and lemon juice. Let it rest a few minutes so the flavors blend.
4. Serve warm in mugs or chilled over ice with an orange slice if you like.

Day 14: Gentle Answer Strategy

"If it be possible, as much as lieth in you, live peaceably with all men."
(Romans 12:18)

The argument started over shoes by the door. It slid fast into old complaints. My voice got louder. His face got tight. We were not talking about shoes anymore. We were talking about being seen, about feeling alone, about a hundred small hurts that never got a soft landing.

Later, with the house quiet, I felt tired and sad. I knew this pattern. Heat rises, words fly, regret follows. I remembered a simple idea I had read and ignored. Prepare one sentence for the next heated moment. Not a script for control, but a rail to hold when emotions wobble.

I wrote mine on an index card and tucked it in the kitchen drawer. "I want to understand you. I can talk when I am calm. Can we pause and try again in ten minutes?" I practiced it out loud so it would be ready when my brain felt scrambled.

It did not take long to test it. The next week the teen rolled his eyes and muttered under his breath. I felt the spark catch. I opened my mouth, then stopped, breathed, and used my sentence. "I want to understand you. I can talk when I am calm. Can we pause and try again in ten minutes?" He shrugged, but the match went out. Ten minutes later, we tried again with lower voices and softer hearts.

Having a gentle sentence did not fix everything, but it changed the weather. It gave me a way to honor Romans 12:18 without pretending that hard things are easy. Peace takes preparation. I started keeping three tools handy. One sentence I could say. One breath I could take. One exit I could choose, like stepping onto the porch for a moment.

We still disagree. We still bump. Yet conflict no longer rules the room. Gentleness does not mean silence. It means strength under control. A prepared sentence helps me bring that strength on time.

Prayer

Spirit, put gentleness on my tongue. Remind me to pause, breathe, and choose words that de-escalate. Give me a ready sentence that honors the person in front of me and keeps the door open for peace. Help our home trade quick heat for steady warmth and wisdom. Amen.

A Moment with God

What short, respectful sentence will I practice for the next conflict?

Day 15: Honor Without Burnout

"Honour thy father and thy mother: that thy days may be long upon the land which the Lord thy God giveth thee." (Exodus 20:12)

When Mom began asking the same question every ten minutes, I knew we had crossed into a new season. I wanted to honor her. She had packed my lunches, prayed over my teenage storms, and cheered at every small win. But after months of doctor visits, pharmacy lines, and midnight phone calls, I felt thin and angry. Caregiver strain is sneaky. It whispers, You should do more, while your body begs for rest.

One afternoon I snapped at a nurse on the phone, then hung up and cried on the kitchen floor. I pictured the fifth commandment and felt a wave of guilt. Then God brought a new sentence to mind. Honor is love with limits. Boundaries sustain service.

So I made a care map on a sheet of paper. I listed tasks and asked which needed me and which did not. Pharmacy delivery could be automatic. My brother could handle insurance calls on Tuesdays. A neighbor from church offered to sit with Mom for two hours on Thursdays, so I could take a walk and buy groceries without rushing. I set a simple rule for myself. No medical calls during work hours. I wrote a gentle script for Mom. "I love you. I will call you after lunch." It felt strange at first, then freeing.

I also looked for joy inside the care. I brought old hymns on my phone and listened with her while we folded towels. She sang every word to "Great Is Thy Faithfulness" though she could not remember what day it was. I held that sound like a jewel.

Honoring parents is not martyrdom. It is faithful love over time. Burnout steals honor. Boundaries protect it. When resentment rose, I checked my map and adjusted. When guilt poked, I asked, Is this real conviction or just fear of disappointing someone? Then I brought it to God and a friend who knows this road.

We are not meant to carry the whole load alone. God gives a body of people and practical tools so that love can last. Sustainable service is still service. It is also wise.

Prayer

Show me sustainable ways to honor and serve. Give me courage to set loving limits, and humility to ask for help. Strengthen my hands for the tasks that are mine, and release the ones that are not. Fill our care with small joys that keep love warm and steady. Amen.

A Moment with God

What one task will I delegate or schedule to care well without resentment?

Day 16: Whatever You Do

"Whatever you do, work at it with all your heart, as working for the Lord, not for human masters." — Colossians 3:23

Monday started with a cold breeze and a to-do list that felt like a cornfield taller than me. My inbox was a tangled patch of weeds. The copier jammed. My coffee tasted like burnt cinnamon. By 10 a.m., I had already sighed my way through three meetings, and I still had "real work" waiting. I wanted a big, meaningful project. Instead, I was staring at scheduling emails, budget updates, and a spreadsheet of tiny numbers that made my eyes cross.

On my walk back from the printer, I passed a coworker's desk. She had a photo of a fall field on her wall, golden and ready. Under it, a small note: "Glean where you are." I thought of Ruth gathering grain at the edges, faithful with what was right in front of her. I felt a nudge. What if I stopped judging my tasks and started offering them?

I opened the spreadsheet and whispered, "Jesus, this is for You." I slowed down enough to catch three small errors. They were tiny, but catching them would save our team money. Next, I answered a handful of emails with warmth instead of speed. I added one extra sentence that cleared confusion. A coworker replied, "Thank you, this helped so much." I took a deep breath. My work had not changed. My aim had.

Around lunch, I cleaned the break room counter. No one saw it. No one clapped. But I pictured setting a small loaf on the table for Jesus. My heart softened. The day felt less like surviving and more like worship. I realized I had been waiting for a different field, a more glamorous harvest. God was inviting me to glean the field I already had, stalk by stalk, email by email, conversation by conversation.

By 3 p.m., I had not finished everything, but I had given

my best to what I touched. The office felt lighter. My soul did too. When my boss stopped by to thank me for the clean numbers, I smiled. It was not about praise. It was about purpose. Working unto Him turned ordinary tasks into offerings. Ordinary became holy right at my desk.

Prayer

Jesus, meet me in my work today. Turn my lists into love and my tasks into worship. Guard my heart from grumbling. Help me see the field I actually have, and glean it with care, joy, and integrity. I offer my hands, my pace, and my attitude to You. Amen.

A Moment with God

Which task, done unto You, would most bless someone by 3 p.m.?

Day 17: Commit, Then Act

"Commit to the Lord whatever you do, and he will establish your plans."
— Proverbs 16:3

Sunday night, my planner looked like a crowded market. Sticky notes layered over meetings, reminders, school pickups, and three big goals that all felt urgent. I color-coded everything, then felt tired just looking at it. My chest tightened. What mattered most? I could not tell.

I set my pen down and prayed, "Lord, I commit this to You." I pictured laying my week on His table like a basket of mixed fruit. Some pieces were bruised. Some were ripe. I asked, "Show me what to drop and what to drive."

On Monday morning, two things shifted. First, I sensed I should cancel a recurring meeting that had turned into a time-waster. It felt risky, but I emailed the group and proposed a monthly check-in instead. Everyone agreed. Second, I realized I needed to step back from a volunteer project I had taken out of guilt. I called the leader and said, "I cannot serve well right now." My voice shook, but peace followed. Like pruning a branch, it stung for a moment, then made room for growth.

With that space, my top two priorities came into focus. I outlined a key report and planned a focused work block for it. I also scheduled two 25-minute sprints to prepare an important client call. Instead of bouncing between tasks, I drove these two. Interruptions still popped up, but I made quicker choices. If it did not serve what God had highlighted, it waited.

By midweek, my list felt lighter, not because it was short, but because it was owned by God. I was no longer carrying the full weight of outcomes. Committing my plans did not mean He did my work. It meant He clarified it. He helped me release the leaves so the fruit could form.

By Friday afternoon, I looked back and saw progress where it counted. Not perfect, but clear. Committing first had turned down the noise and turned up courage. The basket was no longer overflowing. It held what belonged.

Prayer

Direct my steps and prune my list. I give You my plans, energy, and expectations. Cut what is clutter. Strengthen what is fruitful. Teach me to choose what You are blessing and let go of what You are not. Establish my plans as I commit them to You. Amen.

A Moment with God

Which two items will I intentionally not do this week, and why?

Day 18: For His Glory

"So whether you eat or drink or whatever you do, do it all for the glory of God." — 1 Corinthians 10:31

The office felt sleepy that gray morning. Leaves drifted past the window like quiet confetti. My assignment was simple and dull: clean up a database. Thousands of names. Duplicate entries. Typos. No one would cheer. No one would notice unless something went wrong. Part of me wanted to rush, check the box, and move on.

I thought of my grandmother, who used to mend socks by the lamp every autumn. She stitched small holes with steady hands. No one praised her for it. But our feet were warm all winter. Her quiet care revealed God's character. Faithful. Patient. Thorough.

I prayed, "Be glorified in my unseen labor." I slowed to a sustainable pace and built a tiny checklist. Confirm the spelling. Merge duplicates. Note odd patterns. I turned on gentle music and worked like I was tidying a room for a guest. Halfway through, I found a hidden issue that would have caused a billing mistake. Fixing it would save headaches for our team and our clients. I smiled. Glory looks like doing the right thing when no one claps.

Later, a coworker asked how I stay motivated with repetitive tasks. I told her, "I imagine God watching, not to judge, but to delight. I want Him to see His character in my work." She nodded and said she might try it on her next inventory count.

By the end of the day, the database was clean. My name was not on any banner, but peace filled my heart. I realized God uses hidden work to shape hidden places in me. He teaches me to be the same person offstage as on. He trains me to love excellence without an audience. That is worship too.

Autumn is the season of quiet work. Fields do not shout. They stand steady, full of what has grown in secret. When I do small tasks with care, I join that rhythm. I point to a God who sees, who values, who makes ordinary holy.

Prayer

Be glorified in my unseen labor. Form patience in me when tasks repeat. Teach me to reflect Your steadiness, kindness, and truth even when no one is looking. Let my attitude, accuracy, and pace honor You. Use small faithful acts to serve others and shape my heart. Amen.

A Moment with God

What invisible task will I perform excellently today as an offering?

Day 19: Divine Detours

"Jesus stopped and said, 'Call him.'" — Mark 10:49

*M*y plan was airtight. Two focused work blocks, a quick lunch, and an afternoon finish. I even put my phone on do not disturb. At 10:12 a.m., just as I settled into my rhythm, our new intern tapped my door. Her eyes were glossy. "Do you have a minute?"

My first thought was no. I felt that pinch of interruption, like a pebble in my shoe. Then I remembered Jesus on the road, important crowds pressing around Him, and He stopped for one voice. He did not just have a plan. He had people.

I invited her in. She sat on the edge of the chair, twisting a ring. Her project had gone wrong. An email thread had embarrassed her. She wanted to quit. I listened, asked a few questions, and told her about my first months on the job, when I accidentally sent a draft to a client and cried in the bathroom. We laughed. I showed her how to fix the mistake, and we wrote a humble follow-up together.

It took 30 minutes. I lost some momentum, but she walked out taller. A few hours later, she sent me a note: "Thank you for seeing me." I stared at that line. Seeing me. My plan had felt like the assignment. She was the assignment.

That afternoon, another detour came. A neighbor texted that her car would not start. I had dinner to make, but I had a set of jumper cables and ten minutes. We got her car running. My soup simmered a little later. No harm done. My heart felt stretched in a good way.

Not every interruption is holy. Some are distractions, and some can wait. But some are invitations. When I pause and ask, "Lord, is this from You?" I usually sense a gentle yes or a simple no. The yes moments rarely fit my schedule, but they always fit His heart. Jesus stops for people. If I want to walk with Him, I learn to stop too.

Prayer

Help me notice the person, not just the plan. Give me wisdom to discern good interruptions from distractions. Slow my pace enough to see tears, questions, and needs around me. When You say "stop," help me stop. When You say "go," help me go with love and courage. Amen.

A Moment with God

Which interruption today might be the very work You are giving me?

Day 20: Excellence Without Perfection

> *"He has shown you, O mortal, what is good. And what does the Lord require of you? To act justly and to love mercy and to walk humbly with your God."*
> — Micah 6:8

I spent an entire afternoon polishing a presentation. I shifted fonts, moved images, and debated between two shades of orange that looked almost the same. The content was solid by noon. By three, I was still polishing. The deadline slid closer, and my stomach knotted. I was polishing past purpose.

Micah's words came to mind. God asks for justice, kindness, and humility. Not flawlessness. My perfectionism often hides fear, the fear of being judged or missing the mark. Excellence serves people. Perfection serves my pride.

I took a breath and asked, "Who does this need to help, and how?" I wrote a clear story at the top of the slides. I cut two fancy charts that looked smart but did not add value. I checked for accuracy, then set a finish line: stop at 4 p.m., review once, send. When the clock hit four, my hand resisted the mouse, but I clicked send anyway.

The presentation went well. People asked good questions. One teammate said, "I appreciated how simple it was." That felt like grace. Later, I realized the extra hour I would have spent tweaking could be used to help a coworker stuck on a deadline. Excellence freed me to be generous. Perfection would have kept me trapped in my own head.

Autumn reminds me that fruit does not need to be flawless to be good. Apples have specks. Pumpkins have bumps. They still nourish. God is not grading my slides on style points. He is watching how I treat people, how I steward time, how I hold my heart. He loves a humble walk more than a spotless report.

Setting a "good enough" finish line did not lower standards. It focused them. It honored purpose. It gave me space to do the next right thing with a clear mind and a gentle spirit.

Prayer

Keep me faithful, not fussy. Teach me to aim for love, truth, and clarity over spotless details that do not serve anyone. Help me set wise finish lines and stop on time. Make my work excellent because it serves others well and reflects Your heart, not my fear. Amen.

A Moment with God

Where am I polishing past purpose, and what good-enough finish line will I set?

Day 21: Provision on the Plate

"He makes grass grow for the cattle and plants for people to cultivate, bringing forth food from the earth, wine that gladdens human hearts, oil to make their faces shine, and bread that sustains their hearts." — Psalm 104:14–15

The first cold snap came overnight. I woke to a gray sky and a sink stacked with dishes from yesterday's rush. My plan was salad for lunch because I felt guilty about last night's cinnamon rolls. But by noon the wind had teeth, and my body wanted warmth. I opened the fridge and stared at a pot of leftover butternut squash soup, a heel of sourdough, and a small wedge of cheddar. A quiet voice in my head started the usual math. Too many carbs. Too heavy. Be good. Earn it later.

I set the pot on the stove, then paused. The verse I read that morning came back like a gentle hand on my shoulder. God brings forth food from the earth, bread that sustains the heart. Not bread that tests me. Not soup that proves my worth. Provision. Gift.

I ladled the soup, toasted the bread, and sliced a thin square of cheese. Steam curled up in soft ribbons. I tasted sage, sweetness, and a hint of pepper. For the first time in a long time, I received my meal without a courtroom in my head. I simply said, Thank You. I felt my shoulders drop. My stomach unclenched. My mind quieted.

As I ate, I thought about the way God designed seasons. In fall we gather, simmer, and share. Food is not a trap. It is a sign that God sees the body He made, in cooler days and busy weeks. The squash grew from soil God watered. The grain was milled and kneaded by hands He formed. The soup warmed more than my belly. It warmed my attitude.

There are times to choose lighter foods, and there are times to choose hearty bowls that hug the inside of your ribs. Neither is a prize. Neither is a punishment. Both can be prayer. The difference is the heart that receives with thanks.

After lunch, I washed the bowl with hot, soapy water and smiled. I did not need to promise an extra workout to pay for lunch. I needed to remember the table is a place where God meets me, not a test I keep failing. Today, I passed nothing. I received everything.

Prayer

Provider, thank You for today's bread. Teach me to see meals as Your care, not my exam. Bless the hands that grew, carried, and cooked what I eat. Calm the food guilt and fill my heart with gratitude, so every bite becomes praise and every table becomes peace.

A Moment with God

What simple, nourishing meal will I plan that brings peace, not pressure?

Day 22: Brisk Breath, Joyful Steps

"Let everything that has breath praise the Lord." — Psalm 150:6

I used to walk to erase. Erase a cookie. Erase a feeling. Erase the voice that said I was not enough unless I earned it. On a chilly afternoon, I almost skipped my walk because I felt tired and behind. The sky was pale like washed denim, and the trees were shaking loose copper leaves that skittered across the sidewalk. I laced my shoes anyway and told myself it would only be ten minutes.

The first breath burned a little, cold and clean. My cheeks stung, then warmed. A maple leaf landed on my sleeve like a tiny red hand. My phone stayed in my pocket. I did not press start on any tracker. I whispered the verse out loud, timing the words with my steps. Let everything that has breath praise the Lord. In. Out. Praise. Step.

I noticed things I usually miss when I am in task mode. A neighbor's pumpkin with a crooked smile. The soft clap of leaves under my feet. A squirrel scolding me for disturbing his stash. My body felt sluggish when I left the house, but as I moved, my spirit woke up. Movement was not a tax. It was a way to join creation's worship. The wind sang in the pines. My knees creaked a little, then loosened. Even that sound felt like percussion in a simple autumn choir.

I thought about years of using exercise like a judge's gavel. No joy. No wonder I dreaded it. That day, I treated walking like prayer with a beat. I matched my breath to a simple thanksgiving. Thank You for lungs, for legs, for this block, for this blue door, for this crunchy path. Ten minutes slipped by. I wanted ten more, not to earn anything, but to keep praising.

I came home with pink cheeks and a lighter mood. The to-do list was still long, but I felt less trapped under it. Joy had sneaked in through my feet. I poured tea, stretched for two minutes, and smiled at the steam rising like a tiny altar. My steps had not bought me grace. They helped me notice the grace already given.

Prayer

I praise You with my steps. Turn my walks into worship and my breath into a hymn. Free me from earning. Let movement be a gift I unwrap with gratitude, even on busy days and cold afternoons. Meet me on the sidewalk, and steady my pace with Your joy.

A Moment with God

Where will I take a 10-minute leaf walk this week?

Day 23: Bless This Body

"I praise You, for I am fearfully and wonderfully made." — Psalm 139:14

The mirror has been a battlefield for me. On a brisk Saturday, I tried on a sweater I loved last year. It clung in places I wished it would not. A stream of criticism rose fast. Too soft. Too slow. Not enough. I felt the old urge to fix everything at once. New plan. New rules. New me by Friday.

Then I caught my own eyes in the mirror. Tired. Kind. Human. I remembered the verse I learned as a child but rarely used as an adult. Fearfully and wonderfully made. I sat on the edge of the bed, smoothing the sweater's knit between my fingers, and decided to try something new. Bless, not bash.

I pulled out a notebook and wrote a letter, simple and honest. Dear legs, thank you for carrying me up the hill behind our house, even when the wind pushes back. Dear hands, thank you for chopping apples, tying shoes, and holding hot mugs in cold kitchens. Dear skin, thank you for being my first coat in this crisp air. Dear eyes, thank you for catching the gold in the late afternoon light. With each line, my chest loosened.

Stewardship felt different than scrutiny. Stewardship led to care. I filled a glass of water. I put lotion on my shins that always get dry in October. I chose a different sweater that moved with me. I took a slow, kind stretch, not to punish, but to treat this body like a friend I plan to keep.

Gratitude did not make me deny reality. My knees still ache sometimes. My energy dips. My shape has changed. But gratitude changed the story I tell about my body. From problem to partner. From project to place of praise. God did not hand me a mannequin body to display. He gave me a living body to tend.

I walked past the mirror again and smiled without sucking in my stomach. The sweater was just a sweater. My body was not the enemy. Blessing is not vanity. It is agreement with God about what He made. When I bless this body, I treat it like His, on loan to me, worthy of care, ready for purpose.

Prayer

Creator, teach me to honor this body. Quiet the critic and grow the caretaker. Help me speak blessing and choose care that fits this season. Let my thoughts align with Your truth, so my words and habits match love. Thank You for making me, and for not making mistakes.

A Moment with God

Which part of my body will I bless in writing today, and how will I care for it?

Day 24: Drink Deep

"Whoever drinks the water I give them will never thirst." — John 4:14

Autumn air is lovely and sneaky. It feels cool, so I forget to drink. By midafternoon my head pounds, my mouth feels like felt, and my patience is paper thin. I reach for coffee and wonder why I still feel dry. That morning I read Jesus' words about living water. The phrasing tugged at me while I rubbed chapstick on chapped lips and stared at my empty cup.

I set a clear glass on the counter and watched the faucet fill it until light danced across the surface. Simple. Free. Close. I took a long sip and whispered, Jesus, satisfy my thirst within. The water slid down like mercy. I felt a little foolish that I had ignored such an easy help.

I decided to pair sips with short prayers all day. I put a bottle by the sink, another on my desk, and a third in the car cup holder. I taped a tiny note to each one. Come, Living Water. Every time I lifted a bottle, I lifted that prayer. During emails. While folding sweaters. In the school pickup line. My body perked up, and so did my spirit. Hydration is not salvation, but it reminded me to ask for what I need.

In the afternoon, a friend called with heavy news. I listened and walked to the sink. I filled a glass and pictured her name on it. Lord, pour for her too. I could not fix her situation, but I could keep coming to the source. The rhythm steadied me. My headache faded. My heart felt held.

Jesus met a woman at a well on an ordinary day and spoke to her thirst under the thirst. I think of that when I reach for water and want something deeper. He does not shame our needs. He names them and answers them with Himself. I still forget and get cranky. So I set cues. Cup by the coffee maker. Bottle by my Bible. Mug by the bed. The more I drink deep, the less I run on empty.

Prayer

Jesus, satisfy my thirst within. Remind me to drink what my body needs and to ask You for what my soul longs for. As I sip, teach me to pray simple prayers. Pour Your peace into dry places, and make me a small well for others who are weary.

A Moment with God

Where will I place a water cue and a one-line prayer today?

Day 25: A Fiery Sip of Grace

"His word is in my heart like a fire, a fire shut up in my bones. I am weary of holding it in; indeed, I cannot."—*Jeremiah 20:9*

Fall has a way of stirring us awake. The air sharpens, the leaves crackle, and even our bodies feel the shift. It is a season that reminds us that God did not design us for dullness but for renewal and fresh passion. His Word, alive in us, is not a quiet whisper to be tucked away but a fire meant to burn bright, bringing warmth and strength to weary hearts.

Too often, I let that fire cool. The weight of schedules, the sameness of routines, and the discouragement of unmet expectations can leave my soul lukewarm. I tell myself I will get to the Word tomorrow or that one more push in my own strength will be enough. Yet when life grows heavy, I feel the absence of that flame. My heart longs for more than survival. It longs for the fire of God's presence.

Jeremiah's words remind me that God's Word is not passive. It is alive, burning, and unstoppable. Even when Jeremiah tried to stay silent, the Word blazed within him until he could not hold it back. That same holy fire is offered to us today. When we open Scripture, when we worship, when we pray with honesty, God ignites passion where weariness has dulled us. His Spirit fills our bones with strength and His joy with power.

It is the same kind of jolt I taste when Mother's Autumn Zest Fire Cider comes to the table. The vinegar tang, the spice of ginger and peppers, the warmth of honey and garlic are sharp and unforgettable. They wake me up. They do not let me stay sluggish. In the same way, God's Word stirs us, ignites us, and pushes us out of apathy into joy-filled strength. Just as Fire Cider burns away the dullness of the body, God's Word burns away the dullness of the soul.

When I sip it, I remember that passion for the Lord is not something I must create. It is something I receive as His Word works within me like a holy fire shut up in my bones. And once lit, I cannot hold it in. It overflows into encouragement for my family, hope for my friends, and joy that carries me through the season ahead.

Prayer

Lord, let Your Word burn within me like a holy fire. Keep me from living lukewarm or weary. Ignite my heart with passion and joy that cannot be contained, and let it spill into the lives of those around me. Amen.

A Moment with God

Where do I need to let God's Word rekindle passion in me today instead of settling for lukewarm faith?

Autumn Zest Fire Cider

Servings | Prep Time | Cook time
1 Quart   25'   1 month

Fire Cider is a traditional folk tonic created in the fall to boost immunity and bring warmth through the cold months. Drink a spoon, add to teas, marinades or salads.

INGREDIENTS
- 1 cup molasses
- ½ cup fresh ginger, grated
- ½ cup fresh horseradish, grated
- 1 medium onion, chopped
- 10 cloves garlic, crushed or chopped
- 2 jalapeño peppers, chopped
- Zest and juice of 1 lemon
- 2 tablespoons dried rosemary or several sprigs of fresh rosemary
- 1 tablespoon ground turmeric
- Raw apple cider vinegar
- ¼ cup raw honey, plus more to taste

DIRECTIONS
1. Place the ginger, horseradish, onion, garlic, jalapeños, lemon zest, lemon juice, rosemary, and turmeric in a quart-size glass jar.
2. Cover the mixture with raw apple cider vinegar, making sure it rises about two inches above the ingredients.
3. Lay a square of natural parchment or wax paper under the lid, then seal tightly and shake well.
4. Store the jar in a cool, dark place for one month, shaking once each day.
5. After one month, strain through cheesecloth into a clean glass jar, pressing the pulp to release all liquid.
6. Stir in ¼ cup raw honey until dissolved, then taste and add more honey if desired. should taste hot, spicy, and a lil' sweet.

Day 26: The Complaint Fast

"Do not let any unwholesome talk come out of your mouths, but only what is helpful for building others up according to their needs, that it may benefit those who listen." — Ephesians 4:29

It started before sunrise. The coffee tasted weak. The sink was full again. Someone left socks on the stairs, and the dog tracked in mud. I muttered my way through the kitchen, turning tiny annoyances into verbal hills. By school drop-off, my voice had a sharp edge. The car felt heavy with it.

At a red light I caught my reflection. Tired eyes. Tight jaw. I thought of how I had set the tone of our morning with constant grumbling. No one walked out the door taller. I told myself it was harmless, just honesty. But my words did not bring life. They drained it.

At lunch I texted a friend to vent. She wrote back, "Try a complaint fast. One day. Every gripe gets swapped for gratitude." My first reaction was to roll my eyes. Then I looked at the verse taped on my fridge. Ephesians 4:29 stared back. Build up. Benefit those who listen. The Spirit nudged. Try it.

I put a simple plan in place. A hair tie went on my wrist as a cue. Every time I caught a complaint, I would stop, take a breath, and replace it with thanks. "This house is a mess" became "Thank You for a home that holds us." "Why is dinner always my job" became "Thank You for food to share." I told the kids I was trying a challenge. They grinned and joined in by catching me whenever my tone slid.

The first hour felt awkward. Gratitude words came out slow and clumsy. But around dinner, something shifted. Laughter found its way back. Music hummed while we chopped vegetables. The house did not become spotless. The dog still tracked mud. Yet the atmosphere changed because the sound changed.

By bedtime, I realized my words had power I had treated carelessly. Complaining had become a habit that shaped the room. The fast did not silence reality. It redirected it. Replace grumbling with gratitude and the tone of your home will shift. Mine did, in one day.

Prayer

Lord Jesus, guard my mouth and redirect my words. Put a holy pause between thought and speech. Turn complaints into thanks, irritation into blessing, and sarcasm into encouragement. Let my home hear life today, right now. Teach me to build others up so they feel seen, safe, and loved. Amen.

A Moment with God

What phrase will I say instead of my most common complaint?

Day 27: Come Away and Rest

"He said to them, 'Come with me by yourselves to a quiet place and get some rest.'" — Mark 6:31

The calendar looked like a crowded freeway. Practices, meetings, a birthday party, a work deadline, a bake sale sign-up I agreed to at 11 p.m. with sleepy judgment. I could feel it in my shoulders. Short answers. Fast breaths. Joy was being squeezed right out by good things.

On Tuesday afternoon, I sat in the car after another pick-up and thought of Jesus' invitation. He did not say, "Try harder." He said, "Come with Me." I pictured Him pointing not to more hustle but to a quiet place. My quiet place felt imaginary lately. The noise of obligation had taken over my map.

So I did something small and scandalous to my inner perfectionist. I opened my calendar and started pruning. I sent two kind emails to cancel, not with long excuses but with honesty. "I overcommitted. I need to rest this week." I asked a friend to swap carpool. I put a "family night" block across Friday evening in thick ink. It felt like clearing thorny branches to let sunlight reach the ground.

That afternoon, instead of racing to cram one more thing, I walked the neighborhood with no podcast. Just trees, the slap of my shoes, and my pulse slowly dropping. I noticed a maple blushing red at the edges. I whispered, "Thank You." The quiet did not fix my to-do list, but it changed me. I came home softer.

The week did not fall apart. The bake sale had plenty of brownies without mine. My boss appreciated honest communication more than a burned-out employee. The kids did not miss the activity we paused. They loved popcorn and a movie in pajamas. Joy, like a thirsty plant, lifted its head when I cut back the overgrowth.

Pruning is holy. Jesus Himself said to come away. Rest is not lazy. It is obedience. Overfilled weeks starve joy. Make room, and joy grows again.

Prayer

Shepherd of my soul, teach me a restful rhythm. Lead me to quiet places even on busy days. Give me courage to say no kindly, to prune with wisdom, and to trust You with what I release. Fill the space with Your peace, and restore joy to my pace and home. Amen.

A Moment with God

Which commitment will I kindly decline or pause this month?

Day 28: Number Your Days, Not Notifications

"Teach us to number our days, that we may gain a heart of wisdom." —
Psalm 90:12

The ping started before my feet touched the floor. News alerts, sale emails, a reel that made me forget what I got on my phone for in the first place. By noon I had checked my phone dozens of times, then wondered where the morning went. I felt jittery, scattered, thin.

I read Psalm 90:12 and felt a sting. I was numbering notifications, not days. My phone had become a bossy toddler. It shouted, and I obeyed. I did not like who I was becoming. Distracted. Half-listening. Rushing past faces I love to chase a glowing screen.

So I decided on a 24-hour digital prune. Not a dramatic delete of everything. Just clear, gentle boundaries to retrain my attention. I picked two: no phone in the bedroom, and social apps off my home screen. I told my family my plan so they could cheer and check me. I set Do Not Disturb with favorites allowed, then moved the charger to the kitchen.

The first hour my hand reached for a ghost. Muscle memory is real. I kept a small notebook nearby to catch the urge to look something up and to write it down for later. When curiosity calmed, I looked up. The house had a different sound. Quiet, then giggles from down the hall.

In the time I usually scroll, I simmered soup, lit a candle, and sat on the floor to build a puzzle with my kid. I read one chapter of a book that had been waiting. I answered a message that needed thought instead of a heart emoji. By evening, my brain felt less buzzy. The hours did not multiply, but they returned to me.

The next morning I checked my phone with purpose instead of panic. I remembered that wisdom is not anti-technology. It simply puts screens in their proper place. When we number days, we treasure minutes. When we number notifications, we scatter them. I want to live gathered and present.

Digital pruning returns hours to what matters most. Try two boundaries for one day. Watch what comes back.

Prayer

God of time, make me wise with time. Train my attention to love what You love. Quiet the reflex to reach for noise. Help me choose presence over distraction, conversation over scrolling, purpose over autopilot. Teach my hands and heart a better rhythm that honors You and the people near me. Amen.

A Moment with God

Which two phone boundaries will I practice for 24 hours?

Day 29: Birds and Bank Accounts

"Look at the birds of the air; they do not sow or reap or store away in barns, and yet your heavenly Father feeds them. Are you not much more valuable than they?" — Matthew 6:26

Bills sat in a stack like small bricks. Groceries cost more than last month. A surprise repair tapped our savings. I felt tight in my chest. I opened the bank app the way some people check weather, many times a day, hoping the numbers would soothe me. They did not.

I took my coffee to the porch and watched a sparrow hop on the railing. Then a robin. Then a pair of finches at the feeder, chattering like old friends. The verse from Matthew rose to the surface. Look at the birds. Not at the budget spreadsheet first. Look and remember.

God feeds them. They do not fret, even though they do work. They gather what He provides. I realized I had been budgeting with fear, not trust. The plan was about control, not wisdom. I decided to begin again, this time with prayer and a simple step.

I grabbed a notebook and made a calm list. First, gratitude for past provision. Rent paid every month. Side jobs that came right on time. A debt we finished last year. Then one stress-lowering action for this week. We chose a small, smart move: three dinners planned from the pantry and a pause on impulse purchases. I set one auto-transfer to a tiny savings buffer. We scheduled a ten-minute money chat instead of an hour we would dread. We prayed together before we opened the laptop.

Nothing magical happened to our numbers that day. The birds did not deliver cash. But peace perched closer. Fear shrank when trust expanded. With a plan that matched our real life and God's promises, we felt led instead of chased.

Budget with trust, not fear. God feeds and guides. Take one steady step. He cares for sparrows. He cares for you.

Prayer

Father, provide as You promise. Quiet the panic that pushes me to grasp and hoard. Teach me to work with wisdom, to budget with trust, and to notice Your daily care. Lead our choices this week. Give us one clear step that lowers stress and honors You with what we have. Amen.

A Moment with God

What single money step will lower stress this week?

Day 30: Build With Wisdom

"By wisdom a house is built, and through understanding it is established;
through knowledge its rooms are filled with rare and beautiful treasures."
— Proverbs 24:3–4

There was a hotspot in our home that bullied my peace. The kitchen counter collected everything. Mail, keys, headphones, school forms, a screwdriver that no one returned. I would tidy it, then it would swell again. Chaos does not just look messy. It sounds loud inside your head.

One afternoon I decided to stop sighing at it and start small. Ten minutes. Timer on the stove. Music quietly on. I whispered the proverb as the seconds ticked. By wisdom a house is built. Not by shame. Not by a weekend I do not have. By simple, steady choices.

I cleared the surface completely. I wiped it down with warm, soapy water. Then I sorted fast. Trash. Recycle. Return. A small basket for daily essentials only. Keys, wallet, one pen, the charger. I put a folder on the fridge for school papers that used to hover. I made a landing spot by the door for bags and coats. When the timer buzzed, I was surprised. The counter looked different. So did I.

That week, we protected the reset. If something hovered on the counter, I asked myself, Does this belong here? If not, it moved quickly to its home. Ten minutes the next day refreshed the space. The hotspot lost its power to spread. Peace began to collect where clutter had collected before.

I realized our home needs wisdom more than perfection. Wisdom sets a timer and starts. Wisdom chooses one small space and wins it back, again and again. The beauty mentioned in Proverbs does not always mean expensive decor. Sometimes it is clear surfaces, simple systems, and the quiet relief of order.

Ten focused minutes can restore peace to a hotspot at home. Pick one. Reset it. Protect it. Your mind will breathe easier.

Prayer

Lord, bless my home with simple order. Give me wisdom for small steps that make a big difference. Help me start where I am, with what I have, and keep going with grace. Fill our rooms with peace, hospitality, and joy that welcome others and honor You in daily routines. Amen.

A Moment with God

Which small space will I reset today and what timer will I set?

Day 31: Name the Loss

"How long, O Lord? Will you forget me forever?... But I have trusted in your steadfast love; my heart shall rejoice in your salvation. I will sing to the Lord, because he has dealt bountifully with me." – Psalm 13:1–2, 5–6

It started with a shoebox of ornaments on the dining table, the ones we only open when the mornings turn brisk and the trees begin to whisper. I lifted the lid and there it was, the ceramic star we bought the year Mom died. I had tucked it under tissue last December, telling myself I would be braver by now. Instead my chest tightened, and the room felt thin.

All week I had been skirting the edges of sadness. I filled the calendar, baked the first pumpkin bread, said yes to extra projects, and smiled at neighbors raking leaves. But grief is stubborn. It waits until you are holding a memory in your hand and then it asks honest questions: How long, God? How long until this stops aching? How long until the holidays feel light again?

I set the ornament down and finally answered. Out loud. I miss my mother. I miss her laugh while we burned the rolls. I miss the way she hummed hymns while stirring gravy. I miss being someone's daughter in a room full of glittering expectation. Saying it felt like cracking open a window in a stuffy house. The air shifted. Tears came, not as a storm, but like steady rain that waters the ground.

I opened my Bible to Psalm 13 because the psalmist does not pretend. The words made space for mine. David starts with protest and ends with praise. He holds the entire ache and the trust in the same small song. I tried that. I whispered, This hurts. Then I whispered, I still trust Your love. Both were true.

I texted my sister and said, Can we skip the fancy place settings this year and tell one story about Mom instead? She sent back a heart and a yes. It was not a fix, but it felt like a hand finding mine in the dark.

As the sun slid behind the maple, I hung the ceramic star. It looked fragile and brave on the branch. I thought of God not shaming me for my tears, not rushing me through them, but meeting me inside them. The room did not suddenly glow, but it steadied. I could breathe.

That night I wrote two columns in my journal: what I lost and what I still have. I wrote her name on the left and mercy on the right. I did not weigh them. I simply told the truth. Somewhere between the lines, I sensed Him near, not fixing, but faithful. Naming the loss did not shrink it, yet it made room for God to sit with me inside it. I exhaled hope.

Prayer

Father, I bring You grief and trust. Hold both. Receive the tears I cannot name and the ache I finally do. Meet me in honest lament. Steady my heart with Your steadfast love. Teach me to sing again, even softly, because You have dealt bountifully with me, today and tomorrow.

A Moment with God

What loss must I name before I can give thanks?

Day 32: Even If, Yet Rejoice

"Though the fig tree should not blossom, nor fruit be on the vines... yet I will rejoice in the Lord; I will take joy in the God of my salvation. God, the Lord, is my strength; he makes my feet like the deer." – Habakkuk 3:17–19

I was the queen of backup plans until the test results arrived with the same unwelcome word: unchanged. The doctor was kind. The numbers were stable, which should have felt like mercy. Instead it felt like standing at a trailhead with no signposts, just fog, just another appointment circled on a calendar speckled with leaf stickers.

On the way home I stopped at the farm stand for apples. The bins were generous, overflowing, but the owner shook his head when I asked about peaches. "Late frost," he said. "No blossoms took." He said it without bitterness, just as a fact. The trees were there, the roots were deep, but this year the branches could not brag.

In the kitchen I sliced a Honeycrisp and thought of Habakkuk. His words have always felt like the bravest kind of song. Though the fig tree does not bud, though there are no grapes, though the fields fail, yet I will rejoice in the Lord. It is a stubborn joy, not glued to outcomes, anchored to Someone instead of something.

I wanted that. I wanted to rejoice without pretending. So I began small. I thanked God for stable numbers instead of a spiral. I thanked Him for the apple crunch, the way tart can coexist with sweet. I wrote down three things I know about His character even when the harvest is thin: He is near. He is good. He is my strength.

That evening my husband found me on the back steps wrapped in a blanket, staring at the dark outline of the garden. "How are you?" he asked. I told him the truth. Disappointed. Tired of waiting. Still loved by God. We prayed there, not for guarantees, but for grace. The night did not change, but something in me did. My feet felt less like cinder blocks and more like deer hooves finding a ledge.

The next morning I brought a basket to a friend whose pantry is often bare. We laughed in her doorway about applesauce and recipes that stretch. Joy did not crash in like a wave. It arrived like a steady drum, born from trust, beating out a rhythm under everything. Even if the peaches fail, even if the results barely budge, I can still sing because God has not.

He is the same in thin seasons and thick. He will make my feet like a deer's, sure on sharp rock, light where I felt heavy. That promise is not theory. It is oxygen for ordinary days. Outcomes may stall, but God's character does not. On that rock, I rejoice. Even in today's unanswered, I choose stubborn joy here.

Prayer

Lord, even if fruit is scarce, be my strength in the not yet. Anchor my joy to who You are, not to what I see. Make my feet like a deer's on hard places. Train my heart to rejoice, to serve, and to sing while outcomes wait, in Your presence.

A Moment with God

Where will I practice stubborn joy this week despite outcomes?

Day 33: Beauty for Ashes

"...to give them a beautiful headdress instead of ashes, the oil of gladness instead of mourning, the garment of praise instead of a faint spirit..." – Isaiah 61:3

The churn of October had me moving in slow circles, cleaning out the garden beds, clipping brittle stems, and dragging a black bag of dead annuals toward the curb. Everything looked tired. I did too. Grief sat in my body like fog, and disappointment kept stealing my appetite.

I almost missed it. Near the compost bin, a volunteer pansy had popped up, purple with a sunny face, blooming out of the crumbly pile that used to be scraps. I knelt in the damp dirt and laughed. Beauty for ashes, right here beside the trash cans.

Isaiah's promise sounded like poetry when my life was neat. Today it felt practical. God trades what is spent for what is living. He puts a crown where there was coal dust. He drapes praise over a spirit that keeps sighing. Not in fantasy scenes, but in places we think are done.

I carried the pansy to a clay pot and set it on the windowsill above the sink. All afternoon it kept looking at me while I did ordinary chores. It became a little sermon. The banana peels and coffee grounds I toss every day are slowly feeding next spring's tomatoes. The pile of unanswered questions I carry may be the very ground where new tenderness grows.

That evening our small group met. I did not plan to talk, but as the tea steamed and the sky went pink, words tumbled out. I told them about the volunteer pansy, about the ache, about the holidays sneaking toward us without the person we wanted. I expected pity. Instead they passed around a notebook and wrote down one surprising goodness they had noticed that week. Broken dryer, but a neighbor who fixed it for free. Tight budget, but a free pumpkin patch day. Doctor's waiting room, but a conversation that felt holy. We were building a bouquet out of what we thought was debris.

When everyone left, I lit a candle and watched the flame eat the wick. Ash gathered, light stayed. I prayed a simple prayer I did not know I needed: Lord, trade what I cannot carry for what You can grow. I looked at the pansy and believed that God could plant something bright right in the middle of my mess.

The next morning, the air smelled like woodsmoke. I placed a small bowl beside the sink and dropped slips of paper in it through the day, each one a beauty I might have ignored. A child's drawing. A warm mug. A neighbor's wave. The pile grew. Ashes still existed, but so did delight, side by side, and I felt hope waking again.

Prayer

Jesus, open my eyes to hidden beauty. Trade my ashes for what You delight to grow. Plant praise where heaviness sits. Help me notice small wonders within reach and receive them as gifts from Your hand. Make me a planter of hope in tired places, today and this week. Amen.

A Moment with God

What five small beauties are within arm's reach right now?

Day 34: Purpose in Pain

"And we know that for those who love God all things work together for good, for those who are called according to his purpose." – Romans 8:28

The ache did not lift when the plan fell apart. I had circled the retreat on my calendar in ink, three days of quiet by the lake to rest a worn soul. Then the babysitter got sick, the car made a grinding sound, and our savings said a firm no.

Disappointment pressed at my ribs as if to say, See, nothing works. I wanted to argue with it, but I was tired. So I took a long walk instead. The path in the park was slick with leaves, some golden, some rust, all surrendering to the kind of change that does not ask permission. A woman I recognized from church was pushing a stroller and trying not to cry. We met eyes. She stopped. Words poured out. Her husband had left two weeks ago. She had not told anyone.

We sat on a bench. I gave her my last tissue and the little cinnamon muffin I had tucked in my pocket. I listened. That was all. After a while she said, "I asked God for help today." We both looked at the stroller. The baby was asleep and snoring softly. Something holy wrapped the moment like a shawl.

On the way home I thought of Romans 8:28, the verse that can sound like a platitude if you hurl it too fast. Paul does not say everything is good. He says God works all things together for good for those who love Him. Threads, not isolated strands. A Weaver, not a vending machine.

The retreat still did not happen. The car still needed a new part. But my disappointment did not get the final word. God had stitched my no into someone else's yes. He had not removed the ache, yet He had redirected it. That night I heated soup and texted two other women to set up a meal train for the new single mom. Purpose slipped into the house like a quiet guest and sat with us while we wrote our names on the calendar.

I am not grateful for pain. I am grateful that it does not get to be waste. In God's hands, even the scraps can become a quilt, warming someone I did not expect, and me too.

Weeks later, the car was fixed and the leaves were gone. The meal train had become friendship. On a Tuesday afternoon I got a text with a picture of the baby grinning, cheeks like apples. Under it she wrote, "Your no turned into this." I smiled and whispered thanks. The ache still visited, but it had company now, a purpose sitting beside it, weaving good through what remained.

Prayer

Redeemer, weave my pain into purpose. Work all things together for good as I love You and follow Your lead. Do not waste my tears. Use interruptions to serve someone You love. Give me eyes to see the threads You are stitching today, and courage to join You in it.

A Moment with God

What possible good might God be forming through this hardship?

Day 35: Wait With Courage

"Be patient, therefore, brothers and sisters, until the coming of the Lord... See how the farmer waits for the precious fruit... You also, be patient. Establish your hearts." – James 5:7–8

The calendar flipped to November and I felt my shoulders tighten. Waiting wrapped around everything, from slow answers to prayer to a package delayed somewhere between warehouses. Each day ticked toward gatherings I both wanted and dreaded. I wished the season would hurry, then I wished it would pause.

James tells farmers to be patient, to strengthen their hearts as they wait for rain. I do not farm, but I do know a field when I see one. My soul had rows of hope planted and nothing sprouting yet. The temptation was to stare at the dirt and call it failure.

Instead I made a list of small, faithful actions that would not force growth but would welcome it. Seek, serve, sing. Seek God early, even for ten minutes, before my phone asks for my attention. Serve someone quietly, without announcing it. Sing a song of trust when my chest feels hollow.

Day one, I took a short walk in the crisp air and repeated a simple breath prayer: Inhale, You are near. Exhale, I can wait. Later I tucked a grocery card into an envelope for a family in our church. No name, no return address. At dinner I led our home in singing the first verse of "Great Is Thy Faithfulness." We were off-key. It did not matter. The house felt taller.

Day three, the hard thing happened. A message arrived with news I did not want. The soil of my heart clumped and I almost quit the list. Then I thought of the farmer. He cannot yank fruit from branches that are not ready. He tends the ground. He watches the sky. He keeps doing what he knows to do.

So I kept going. I sought God by reading James again. I served by washing dishes before anyone noticed. I sang softly while folding laundry, a thin melody over the rumble. The situation did not change, but I did. Courage slipped in, not as a roar, but as a steadying hand that said, Keep going, the rain is on its way.

By the weekend, I was not magically better. I was grounded. Waiting had become less about clock-watching and more about abiding. Seeking, serving, and singing did not buy a blessing. They kept my heart open to the God who brings fruit in season.

Like the farmer, I cannot rush the clouds, but I can prepare the soil. I can keep short accounts, show up to prayer, bless a neighbor, and hum a hymn while I wash the cups. This is courage in the waiting: faithful steps that say, I believe rain will come, in God's time.

Prayer

Lord, strengthen my heart as I wait. Teach me to wait like a farmer, preparing the soil while You send the rain in season. Help me seek You, serve someone, and sing the truth today. Keep my hope steady and my hands faithful until the harvest comes, by Your grace.

A Moment with God

What two faithful actions can I do while I wait?

Day 36: Blessed to Bless

"I will bless you, and you will be a blessing." (Genesis 12:2) "He supplies seed to the sower and bread for food, and will enlarge your harvest so you can be generous." (2 Corinthians 9:10-11)

It started with two heavy bags of apples on my doorstep, still cool from my neighbor's tree. She texted, "Too many. Please take some." I pulled them inside, shut the door, and felt something I did not expect. I felt protective. My first thought was not recipes or friends to share with. It was a quiet fear inside that said, Keep them. You never know.

That voice felt familiar. It showed up after long months of isolation and tight budgets. It told me to play it safe, to keep my head down, to think small. I rinsed an apple and bit into it, crisp and sweet, juice running down my wrist. The taste woke up a better memory. God called Abraham blessed to be a blessing, not a dead end. Paul said God gives seed and bread, and multiplies both so we can share. Seed is for planting, bread is for eating. Neither is for hoarding.

I pulled out a mixing bowl and started peeling. The kitchen filled with cinnamon and butter. While the loaves baked, I felt my heart soften. I wrote three names on sticky notes. Mrs. Turner down the street, who lost her husband in the spring. Tasha, a single mom from church whose calendar is full and fridge is not. And Marco, the mail carrier who always waves. It felt small. It also felt exactly right.

I wrapped a warm loaf for Mrs. Turner, tucked a card into Tasha's, and set out a slice with a napkin for Marco. I carried the first loaf to Mrs. Turner's porch. She opened the door in her cardigan and slippers, eyes watery. "I was just making tea," she said. "Would you sit with me?" We talked about leaves changing and the way the afternoons feel longer now. When I left, the ache of my own loneliness had lifted a little.

Tasha texted later, "How did you know? I needed this today." Marco left a thank-you note in our mailbox. The apples became more than bread. They became connection. Sharing broke the grip of my fear. I realized God is not trying to take from me. He is trying to move through me. Blessing is both seed and bread. When I plant it in someone's life, there always seems to be more to slice and share.

Prayer

Father, You are the giver of seed and bread. Make me a conduit, not a cul-de-sac. Loosen my grip on what I have. Multiply what I offer. Send me to the lonely, the hungry, the overlooked. Let Your generosity flow through my hands today. Use my home and car. Amen.

A Moment with God

Who will I bless within 48 hours and how?

Day 37: Simple Fall Hospitality

"Practice hospitality." (Romans 12:13) "After you gather the fruit, celebrate before the Lord." (Leviticus 23:39)

I almost canceled. The house felt too small, the baseboards were dusty, and the soup recipe looked... ambitious. My heart raced as I pictured awkward silence and forced smiles. Hospitality used to feel like joy. After a long stretch of isolation, it felt like a test I could fail.

I stood in the kitchen staring at my messy counter and prayed, "Lord, open my door and my heart." An idea as simple as a leaf falling floated in. Tea, soup, open chair. No fancy centerpiece. No five-course meal. Just warmth and presence.

I shifted the plan. I put a pot on the stove and sautéed onions in butter until the kitchen smelled cozy. I chopped carrots and potatoes, added broth, a bay leaf, a handful of lentils. I tossed a tart-sweet apple crisp in the oven because apples were on sale. I did not scrub the grout. I lit one candle and threw a soft blanket over the sofa. I set out mismatched mugs, spoons in a mason jar, and a basket of bread.

When Mia arrived, she laughed at the dog hair on her jeans and hugged me tight. "Your house smells like comfort," she said. My neighbor Kay knocked five minutes later, cheeks pink from the cold. We carried bowls to the table and kept our phones in a basket by the door. The soup was simple, thick, and steaming. Conversation, slow at first, found its rhythm.

We talked about the changing trees and kids starting new schedules. We asked each other, "What was one good thing from this week, and one hard thing?" The answers were raw and real. Kay's good thing was her new job. Her hard thing was fear that she would not keep up. Mia's

good thing was sleep after a season of anxiety. Her hard thing was the silence of her empty nest. We laughed, we listened, we prayed a short prayer that felt like a hand on a shoulder.

No one cared about dust on the bookshelf. We cared about being seen. When they left, the house felt bigger, not because it was cleaner, but because love had stretched it. The feast in Leviticus was not about perfect plates. It was about remembering God together. I can do that with tea and soup and an open chair.

Prayer

Lord, open my door and my heart. Trade my fear of hosting for a love of welcoming. Make my table a place of rest, not performance. Help me notice who needs a warm bowl and a warm smile. Use simple things to carry Your presence into my home. Amen.

A Moment with God

What one simple act of hospitality will I plan this week?

Day 38: Seasoning Words with Hope

"Death and life are in the power of the tongue." (Proverbs 18:21)

The kitchen always felt different when Moravian cookies were on the counter. Paper thin, spiced, and crisp, they carried hope that sweetness could break into even the coldest winter. My grandma always slipped cardamom into the dough, a Persian touch from her childhood. She said it was the spice that made ordinary things shine, and as the fragrance filled the oven, I believed her.

Not every memory was as warm. One holiday the house filled with complaints. The cookies were too dark, the stew too salty, the sugar bowl nearly empty. I could feel the heaviness pressing in. Proverbs 18:21 came to mind. Death and life are in the power of the tongue. Grandma, usually quick to laugh, grew quiet, and I saw how easily careless words could drain the spirit more than a burnt tray ever could.

Later, while rolling dough, she showed me why she loved cardamom. "It is just a seed," she said, grinding it gently, "but it changes everything around it. That is what your words can do too." Her lesson sank deep. Just as a pinch of cardamom transforms plain spice into something memorable, one word of blessing can lift an entire table.

Now when I bake these cookies, I remember her wisdom. The dough is stiff and the rolling hard, but the fragrance rising from the oven reminds me that I can choose what my words will season. From our kitchen table to yours, I have written the recipe on the next page. May each bite remind you to season your life and your words with hope.

Prayer

Lord, set a guard over my lips. Let my words be like cardamom, small but powerful enough to change the atmosphere. Teach me to plant life, not death, and let my table always carry the fragrance of Your goodness. Amen.

A Moment with God

Who needs one specific, affirming sentence from me today?

Your feedback is a true blessing!

If this book has encouraged you or helped you feel less alone, would you leave a quick review?

Even one sentence makes a huge difference and takes just a minute. As a small author, your feedback not only lifts my heart… it also helps other women of faith with find the support and hope they need.

Thank you for being part of this journey!

Scan this QR code with your phone to go to the review page

Or

Go to your orders, find the book and click

"Write a product review"

Thank you <3

Day 39: Remember and Tell

"I will remember the deeds of the Lord. I will ponder all Your work and meditate on Your mighty acts." (Psalm 77:11-12)

Autumn brings with it a special kind of hope. The golden leaves, the crisp air, and the glow of candles or lamps remind us to slow down and notice the blessings that surround us. God gives us this season as a reminder that change can be beautiful and that His presence remains steady through every turn of the year.

Yet it is easy to lose sight of His goodness. Worries often pile up until they drown out gratitude. A forgotten appointment, an unanswered prayer, or a heavy to-do list can cloud the heart with discouragement. Faith can feel thin, and the noise of life can make it hard to recall the ways God has already been faithful.

The psalmist teaches us to resist that forgetfulness by remembering. Psalm 77 shows us that looking back to God's mighty works revives our hope for today. When we pause to name His gifts, whether large or small, we begin to see how much He has carried us through. Remembering is not a backward glance but a practice that strengthens us to walk forward with peace.

This is why our family loves the tradition of baking Moravian cookies in the fall. The thin, spiced cookies fill the house with the fragrance of cinnamon and clove, wrapping us in warmth as we gather around the kitchen. Sharing them reminds me of sharing testimony. Both are small, simple gifts that bring joy, comfort, and strength. Just as the cookies spread sweetness through the house, remembering God's goodness spreads gratitude through our hearts.

So today I encourage you not only to write down a few ways God has been faithful but also to try a batch of Moravian cookies for yourself. Bake them, share them, and let the fragrance remind you of God's nearness. Each bite can be a sweet reminder that His mercies are new every morning and worth telling again and again

Prayer

Lord, help me remember Your goodness when my heart forgets. Teach me to see Your faithfulness in small daily gifts and give me the courage to share them with others. May my words and actions spread the warmth of Your presence like the fragrance of cookies in the kitchen. Amen.

A Moment with God

What testimony of God's faithfulness can I write and share this week?

Cozy Moravian Cookies

100 Cookies	95'	5'
Servings	Prep Time	Cook Time

Nutritional Info (per serving)
Calories: 455 kcal | Protein: 4 g|
Sodium: 249 mg | Fat: 14 g | Carbs: 85 g
| Cholesterol: 23mg

INGREDIENTS
- ½ cup light brown sugar (packed)
- ¾ tsp baking soda
- ½ tsp salt
- ¾ tsp ginger
- ¾ tsp cloves
- ¼ tsp Cardamom
- ¾ tsp cinnamon
- ¼ tsp allspice
- 1 cup molasses
- ½ cup shortening
- 4 cups all-purpose flour

DIRECTIONS
1. In a medium bowl, whisk together the sugar, baking soda, salt, and all spices until well blended; set aside.
2. In a medium saucepan, heat the molasses just to the point of bubbling, but do not let it boil. Stir in the shortening until completely smooth, then cool
3. Transfer the molasses mixture to a stand mixer (or use a hand mixer) and beat in the sugar–spice mixture. Add flour gradually until the dough comes together sticky, then turn onto a floured counter and knead in more flour until very stiff, about 3½ cups total.
4. Shape the dough into a ball, wrap well, and refrigerate until firm; overnight is ideal for handling.
5. Preheat the oven to 375°F (190°C) and line baking sheets with parchment. Roll portions of dough paper-thin on a floured surface, cut into 2-inch circles with a fluted cutter, and transfer with an offset spatula, brushing away excess flour.
6. Arrange cookies close together as they do not spread, and bake one tray at a time: 4 minutes, rotate, then 2 more minutes until crisp. Cool on the sheet, stack, and repeat with remaining dough.
7. They bake and cool really fast

Day 40: Look Up, Fields Are White

"Lift up your eyes and see that the fields are white for harvest." (John 4:35)
"We plan our way, but the Lord establishes our steps." (Proverbs 16:9)

My planner was open, pages neat and bossy. I love fresh ink and tidy boxes. After a season that felt uncertain, I wanted a solid plan for what was next. Career choices. Family rhythms. Ministry ideas. I tried to map it all. The more I wrote, the tighter my chest felt.

I needed air. I grabbed a scarf and walked to the park. The afternoon light was pale gold, the kind that makes everything look kissed by honey. Along the path, white asters bloomed in drifts, small and bright. They looked like tiny flags waving me closer. I heard Jesus' words in my heart. Look up. Fields are white.

I stopped on a wooden bridge and watched leaves swirl in the creek. My plans are not wrong, I thought. They just are not the point. I hold the pen. God holds the page. The harvest is not somewhere far away. It is here, in neighbors, family, coworkers, the barista who knows my order, the kid who cuts across our lawn. The field is ready. My job is to look up and step in, one obedient move at a time.

I sat on a bench and asked God for three practices from these forty days to carry forward. The answers came like stepping-stones. First, a daily blessing. Share one thing, one word, one act. Second, a daily remember. Write one line in the Harvest Log. Third, a daily look up. Ask, "Who is in front of me right now, and how can I love them?"

Back home, I penciled those three into my planner, not as heavy rules, but as rhythms. I left margins open on purpose. I wrote, "Interruptible." That night, an unexpected text came from a friend passing through town. "Any chance you can talk?" In the past, I would have protected my schedule. This time, I looked up. I made tea. We sat in the glow of one lamp and named God's kindness. It felt like a firstfruit of the next season.

Planning with humility did not make me passive. It made me peaceful. I can move forward with a light grip, eyes up, heart ready. The Lord will establish my steps. The fields are white. The harvest is His. I get to be part of it.

Prayer

Establish my steps for Your glory. I offer You my calendar, my goals, and my gaps. Teach me to plan with open hands. Help me notice ripe moments around me today. Keep my eyes lifted and my heart soft. Lead me into the good works You prepared for me. Amen.

A Moment with God

Which three daily practices from this book will I carry into the next forty days?

Your Journey Continues!

Congratulations on finishing these forty days of devotion. You took time to meet with God, to pray, and to grow, and that choice will keep bearing fruit in your life.

If this devotional was a gift, remember how much someone cared about you when they placed it in your hands. If you purchased it for yourself, celebrate the fact that you chose to invest in your walk with God. And now you can consider passing that same encouragement on by giving this book as a gift to someone you love.

Do not forget the easter eggs hidden throughout these pages. If you found them all, email us at contact. greenhopex@gmail.com

and we will send you early access to our next books.

Finally, this devotional is just one step. Be sure to visit our author page to explore more meaningful and beautiful devotionals designed to keep you encouraged in every season

www.ingramcontent.com/pod-product-compliance
Lightning Source LLC
Chambersburg PA
CBHW071533120626
46550CB00006B/2435